I0026888

INDIAN POTTERY

OF THE

SOUTHWEST

A SELECTED BIBLIOGRAPHY

MARCIA MUTH

Sunstone Press
Santa Fe, New Mexico

For Allene F. Schnaitter

Longtime Friend and Professional Colleague

Drawings by Betsy James.

Copyright © 1990 by Marcia Muth.

All Rights Reserved. No part of this book may be reproduced in any form or by any electronic or mechanical means including information storage and retrieval systems, without permission in writing from the publisher, except by a reviewer who may quote brief passages in a review.

FIRST EDITION

Printed in the United States of America

Library of Congress Cataloging in Publication Data:

Muth, Marcia, 1919-
  Indian pottery of the southwest: a selected bibliography / Marcia Muth. – 1st ed.
    p.   cm.
  "A Southwestern Arts Institutes book."
  Includes bibliographical references.
  ISBN: 0-86534-067-6 : $6.95
  1. Indians of North America–Southwest, New–Pottery–Bibliography. 2. Indians of North America–Southwest, New–Antiquities–Bibliography. 3. Southwest, New–Antiquities–Bibliography. I. Title.
Z1209.2.U52S685   1990
(E78.S7)
016.7383'089'97079–dc20   90-9870
                                                                            CIP

Published in 1990 by SUNSTONE PRESS
                 Post Office Box 2321
                 Santa Fe, NM 87504-2321/ USA

TABLE OF CONTENTS

SANTA CLARA JAR

Polish black with indented "bear paw".
11-5/8 inches high, 14-1/8 inches diameter.
Collections of the Museum of New Mexico.

INTRODUCTION

Pottery has been a part of man's life since early times. Primitive peoples made storage jars out of sun-dried clay as well as gourds, skins and baskets. Pottery use usually depended upon there being a close source of clay. Later, firing pottery became common and vessels could also be used to store liquids.

The desire to decorate seems to be an inate one possessed by all peoples. Even the earliest pottery was decorated in some fashion. Sometimes a design was scratched on the raw clay with a stick or fingers were used to produce a symmetrical, repeated image. Painted designs have also been in use from ancient times to the present.

Native American pottery has flourished in the Southwest area. It is believed that pottery making came into the area from the south sometime in the third century BC. It was probably introduced by the Hohokam tribe who moved into what is now Southern Arizona.

The Mogollan culture in New Mexico is known for the production of Mimbres pottery during the eleventh and twelfth centuries. Mimbres pottery which continues to inspire today's potters was known for its black and white decoration. The decorations depicted animal, human and insect shapes.

Unlike some other art forms, pottery in the Southwest has built on the past while still being innovative. Thus it is possible to trace the lineage of a twentieth-century pot back to its earliest beginnings. The purpose of making pottery may have changed but not the inspiration for making it beautiful.

Southwestern pottery has been divided into Prehistoric (300BC-1300AD); Protohistoric (1300-1700); Historic (1700-1875) and Modern (1875-   ). It might also be fitting to add another period — Tourist (1930-   ).

Indian pottery is still made in the same time — honored way

— by hand, using the coiling and scraping method. Designs, incised or painted are based primarily on traditional legends or are symbolic designs. Chewed yucca stalk brushes and polishing stones are still used.

Pottery making was once considered to be solely the province of women. It was they who gathered the clay, shaped, decorated and fired the pots or figures. It was women who then used them in the household or, in later times, bartered or sold them for other household necessities. Now pottery is made by men as well as women.

There have been other noticeable changes. The most evident is that whereas pottery was formerly made for utilitarian or ceremonial use, it is now a viable commodity made for sale to others. Purchasers can be shopkeepers, collectors, museums or tourists. While some pottery is obviously made for the transient tourist trade, most potters are interested in preserving their heritage of artistic excellence.

Another change has been the emergence from anonymity of the Indian potter. Traditionally, potters were not known as individuals only as members of a tribe or Pueblo. However, the enthusiasm and interest of collectors in the works of a particular potter resulted in the knowledge and promotion of individual potters. One of the first to make a personal name for herself and her work as an international artist was Maria Martinez. Her renown led to the recognition of other outstanding Southwestern potters such as Margaret Tafoya, Joseph Lonewolf and Helen Cordero. Today there are many outstanding, well-known and collectible Native Americans who are making pots and figures such as the storyteller dolls.

Contemporary designs may be more reflective of the old legends than exact copies. There is a special vitality to much of contemporary pottery that seems to combine the classical past with its impressive legacy of artistic excellence with the freedom of modern expressionism. For the best potters, the making of pottery is also an act of spirituality.

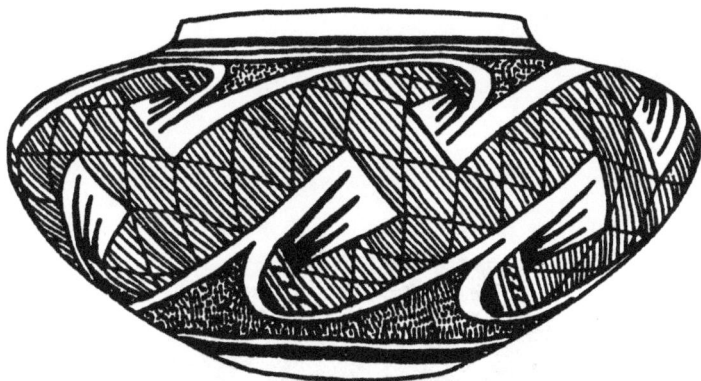

HOPI POLOYCHROME JAR

Black and red on yellow. 3-1/4 inches high, 6-1/2 inches diameter.
Made by Daisy Nampeyo. Collections of the Museum of New Mexico.

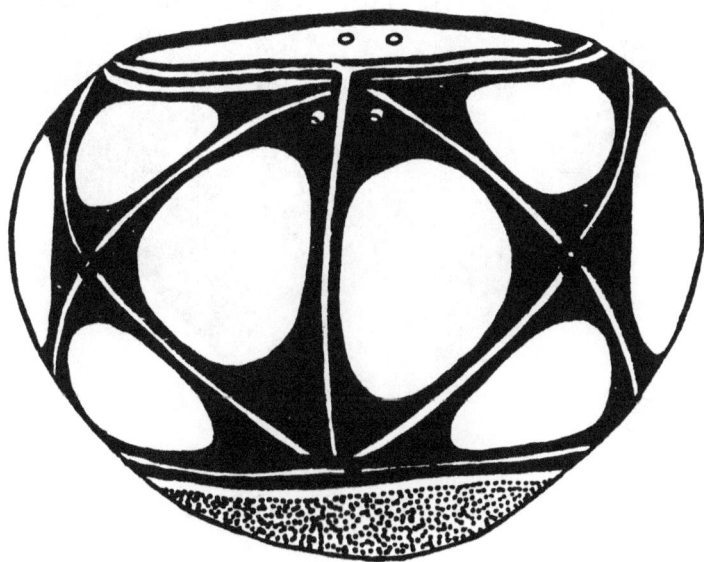

SANTO DOMINGO CLOSED BOWL

Black on white geometric design with line-break; orange-red base.
Holes beneath rim for suspension. Made by Monica Silva. 6-1/4 inches high,
10 inches diameter. Collections of the Museum of New Mexico.

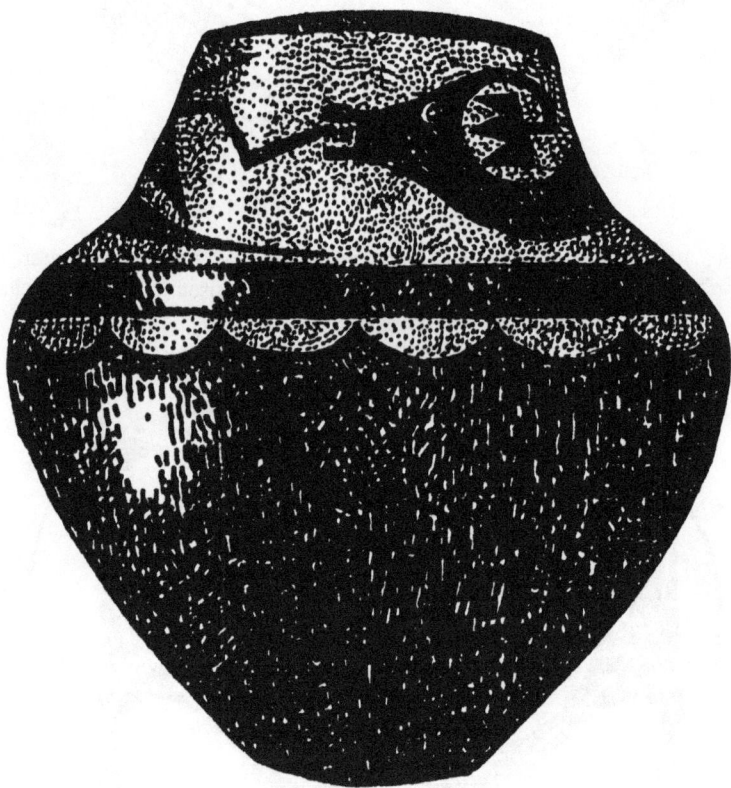

SAN ILDEFONSO JAR

Matte black on polished black. Plummed serpent design.
Made by Tonita Roybal.
11 inches high, 12-1/4 inches diameter.
Collections of the Museum of New Mexico.

A

Allen, Kenneth. "Camera touring in New Mexico . . . the pottery makers." *New Mexico Magazine*, 19:3 (March, 1941): 18-19.

Allen, Laura Graves. *Contemporary Hopi pottery.* Flagstaff: Museum of Northern Arizona Press, 1984.

Amsden, Charles A. *An analysis of Hohokam pottery design.* Globe, AZ: 1936 Medallion papers, No. 23.

Appleton, Leroy H. *American Indian design and decoration.* New York: Dover 1971.

——————.*Indian Art of the Americas.* New York: Scribner, 1950.

Arizona Highways, (entire issue) 50:5 (May, 1974).

Arnold, David L. "Pueblo pottery, 2,000 years of artistry." *National Geographic* 162:5 (Nov., 1982): 593-605.

Austin, Mary. *Indian pottery of the Rio Grande.* Pasadena: Esto Pub. Co., 1934.

B

Babcock, Barbara A. "Clay changes: Helen Cordero and the Pueblo storyteller." *American Indian Art* 8(2). (Spring, 1983): 30-39.

——————.*et al The Pueblo Storyteller: development of a figurative ceramic tradition.* Tucson: University of Arizona, 1986.

Bacon, Lucy. "The Indian as an artist" *New Mexico Highway Journal* 9:11 (Nov., 1931): 29-30,46.

Bahti, Tom *An introduction to Southwestern Indian arts and crafts.* Flagstaff, AZ; KD Publications, 1964.

Ball, Eve. "The potter of Santa Clara" *New Mexico Magazine* 33:2 (Feb, 1955): 25,44. Article about Teresita Naranjo.

Barnes, Scott. "Margaret Tafoya, potter." *The Santa Fean* 13:7 (Aug. 1985): 39-41.

Barry, John. *American Indian pottery: an identification and value guide.* Florence, Al.: Books Americana, 1981.

_____ . _____ . 2d. ed. 1984.

Batkin, Jonathan. "Martina Vigil and Florentino Montoya: master potters of San Ildefonso and Cochiti Pueblos." *American Indian Art* 12 (4): (1987): 28-37.

_____ .Pottery of the Pueblos of New Mexico, 1700-1940. Colorado Springs, CO.: Taylor Museum of the Colorado Springs Fine Arts Center, 1987.

"A beginner's guide to Indian arts and crafts" *New Mexico Magazine* 48: 9-10 (Sept.-Oct., 1970): 10-17.

Bennett, James O'Donnell. "Indian potters create marvels at World Fair." *New Mexican* (July 16, 1934).

Berlant, Tony. "Mimbres pottery: An artist's perspective." *Arizona Highways* 60:1 (Jan., 1984): 24-31.

Bice, Richard A. *Prehispanic pueblo pottery.* Albuquerque: Museum of Albuquerque and Albuquerque Archaeological Society (nd).

Blair, Mary Ellen and Lawrence Blair. *Margaret Tafoya: a Tewa potter's heritage and legacy.* Flagstaff, AZ.: Northland Press, 1985.

Bowen, Gertrude C. "Artists in ancient crafts" *New Mexico Magazine* 27:4 (April, 1949): 11, 42-44.

Breternitz, David A. *An appraisal of tree-ring dated pottery in the Southwest.* Tucson, Az.: University of Arizona, 1966. Anthropological papers No. 10.

Brody, J. J. *Mimbres painted pottery*. Santa Fe: School of American Research and Albuquerque: University of New Mexico Press, 1987.

_____.et al *Mimbres pottery: ancient art of the American Southwest*. New York: Hudson Hills Press in association with The American Federation of Arts, 1983.

_____."Southwestern American Indian pottery, a living tradition." *American Art & Antiques* 2:5 (Sept.-Oct. 1979): 110-117.

Brugge, David M. *Navajo pottery and ethnohistory*. Window Rock, AZ.: Navajo Tribal Museum, 1963. Navajo publications, series 2.

Bunzel, Ruth L. *The pueblo potter, a study of creative imagination in primitive art*. New York: Columbia University Press, 1929. Columbia University Contribution to Anthropology, Vol. 8.

_____._____. Rev. ed. New York: Dover, 1972.

C

Cameron, S. M. "Pueblo pots — for thirteen cents." *New Mexico Magazine* 55:5 (May, 1977): 38-39, 47-48. About the Pueblo pottery postage stamps.

Canfield, Kenneth. "Pueblo pottery reviewed." *The Indian Trader* (Jan. 1978)

Challem, Jack Joseph. "A Black bowl from New Mexico." *New Mexico Magazine*. 58:7 (Sept., 1980): 14-21.

Chapman, Kenneth M. "America's most ancient art." *School Arts Magazine* 30:7 (March 1931): 387-402

_____."Bird forms in Zuni pottery decoration" *El Palacio* 24:2, (Jan. 14, 1928):23-25.

_____ ."Birds from Zuni pottery." *School Arts Magazine* 28:1, (Sept., 1928): 99-100.

_____ .*Indian pottery.* New York: Exposition of Indian Tribal Arts, 1931.

_____ ."Life forms in Pueblo pottery decoration" *Art and Archaeology* 13:3 (1922): 120-122.

_____ ."Post Spanish Pueblo pottery." *Art and Archaeology* 23:5, (1927): 207-213

_____ .*The pottery of San Ildefonso Pueblo.* Albuquerque: Published for the School of American Research by the Univ. of New Mexico Press, 1970 (reprinted 1977). Supplementary text by Francis H. Harlow. School of American Research, Monograph Series No. 28.

_____ .*The pottery of Santo Domingo Pueblo, a detailed study of its decoration.* Santa Fe, NM: Laboratory of Anthropology, 1936, 1938.

_____ ."Pueblo feather designs." *El Palacio* 23:1 (1927): 2-7.

_____ .*Pueblo Indian pottery.* Nice, France: C. Szwedzicki, 1933. Vol. 1.

_____ .*Pueblo Indian pottery of the Post-Spanish period.* Santa Fe, NM: Laboratory of anthropology, 1945.

_____ ._____ . 3rd ed. - 1950.

_____ ."Roadside shopping." *New Mexico Magazine.* 14:6 (June, 1936): 20-21, 38-39.

Chapman, Kenneth M. and Bruce Ellis "The line break, problem child of Pueblo pottery." *El Palacio* 58 (1951): 251-89.

Ciesla, Bill. "Third generation is charm for Jemez potters." *The Indian Trader* 10:12, (Dec. 1979)

Coe, Ralph T. *Lost and found traditions:* Native American Art, 1965-1985. Seattle: Univ. of Washington, 1986.

Collins, John E. *A tribute to Lucy M. Lewis, Acoma potter.* Fullerton, CA; Museum of North Orange County, 1975. Catalog published for the Lucy M. Lewis show, Sept. 27 -Nov. 30, 1975.

Colton, Harold S. "Primitive pottery firing methods." *Plateau* 11 (Apr., 1939): 63-66.

Colton, Harold S. and Hargrave, Lyndon L. *Handbook of Northern Arizona pottery wares.* Flagstaff, AZ.; Museum of Northern Arizona, 1937. Bulletin No. 11.

Corpstein, Alice and Paca, Robert. *Alice Corpstein's windows of the west.* Phoeniz, AZ.: ARS Publishing, 1987.

Cushing, Frank Hamilton. *A study of Pueblo pottery as illustrative of Zuni culture growth.* Washington: Bureau of American Ethnology. 1886. pp 467—521, Fourth annual report.

D

Danson, Edward Bridge and Wallace, R.M. "A petrographic study of Gila polychrome" American Antiquity 22 (1956): 180-183.

Dedera, Don. *Artistry in clay, contemporary pottery of the Southwest.* Flagstaff, AZ.: Northland Press, 1985.

DeWald, Louise. "One family of potters" New Mexico Magazine 56:4 (April, 1978): 30-33, 38, 44-45.

Dickens, Elizabeth. "Shopping for souvenirs." *New Mexico Magazine* 18:8 (Aug. 1940): 12-13.

Dillingham, Rick. "Historic and contemporary Pueblo pottery." *El Palacio* 93:1 (Summer/Fall, 1987): 26-29.

_____ ."The pottery of Acoma Pueblo" *American Indian Art Magazine* 2:4 (1977): 44-51.

_____ .*The red and the black: Santa Clara pottery by Margaret Tafoya.* Santa Fe: Wheelwright Museum, 1983.

Dittert, Alfred E. and Plog, Fred. *Generations in clay; Pueblo pottery of the American Southwest.* Flagstaff, AZ.: Northland Press in Cooperation with the American Federation of Arts, 1980. "This book was published in conjunction with the exhibition, *Generations in clay* ... which was organized by the American Federation of Arts."

Dockstader, Frederick J. *Indian Art in America.* Greenwich, Conn.: New York Graphic Society, 1961.

Douglas, Frederic H. *Hopi pottery.* Pasadena: Esto, 1933.

_____ .*Modern Pueblo pottery types.* Denver: Denver Art Musuem, 1933. Leaflet: 53/54.

_____ .*Pottery of the Southwestern tribes.* Denver: Denver Art Museum, 1935. Leaflet: 69/70.

_____ .*Pueblo Indian pottery making* Denver: Denver Art Museum, 1930. Leaflet No. 6.

_____ .*Seven Navajo pots.* Denver: Denver Art Museum, 1937. Material Culture Notes No. 3

Douglas, Frederic H. and D'Harnoncourt, Rene. *Indian art of the United States.* New York: Museum of Modern Art, 1941.

_____ ._____ . 2nd. ed. 1948.

Douglas, Frederic H. and Raynolds, F. R. "Pottery design terminology." *Newsletter, Clearing House for Southwestern Museums* 35 (1941).

Dutton, Bertha P. *Indians of the American Southwest.* Englewood Cliffs, N.J.: Prentice-Hall, 1975.

E

Eby, Maurice. "A great tradition in pottery." *New Mexico Magazine* 40:4 (April, 1962): 12-13.

_____."The hands of Maria," *New Mexico Magazine* 45:8 (Aug., 1967): 29-31.

Ellis, Florence Hawley. "Historic middle Rio Grande pottery and potters." *Archaeological Paper of New Mexico*. Paper No. 8, 1983.

_____."On distinguishing Laguna from Acoma polychrome." *El Palacio* 73:31 (Autumn, 1966): 37-39.

Evans, Mary. "The Southwest Indian" *American Home* 73:3 (March, 1970): 76-80.

Exposition of Indian Tribal Arts, Inc. *Introduction to American Indian Art*. (New York: 1931) "To accompany the first exhibition of American Indian Art selected entirely with consideration of esthetic value."

F

Fane, Diana. "Curator's choice: Indian pottery of the American Southwest." *American Indian Art Magazine* 11:2 (Spring, 1986): 46-53.

Farrington, William. *Prehistoric & historic pottery of the Southwest: a bibliography*. Santa Fe, NM: Sunstone Press, 1975.

Feder, Norman. *American Indian Art*. New York: Abrams, 1971.

_____.*Two hundred years of North American Indian Art*. New York: Praeger, 1972.

Fewkes, Jesse Walter. *Additional designs on prehistoric Mimbres pottery*. Washington, DC: Smithsonian Institution, 1924.

_____ ."Ancient Zuni pottery." New York: Putnam Anniversary Volume (1909): 43-82.

_____ ."Animal figures on prehistoric pottery from Mimbres Valley, New Mexico." *American Anthropologist, N.S.* 18:4 (1916).

_____ ."Clay figurines made by Navajo children." *American Anthropologist.* 25 (1923): 559-563.

_____ .Designs on prehistoric Hopi pottery. Washington: Bureau of American Ethnology, 1919.

_____ ._____. New York: Dover, 1973.

_____ ."Designs on prehistoric pottery from Mimbres Valley, New Mexico." *Smithsonian Miscellaneous Collections* 44:6 (1923).

Field, Clark. *Indian pottery of the Southwest post Spanish period.* Tulsa: Philbrook Art Center, 1958. "This brochure is designed as an introduction to the Clark Field collection of Indian pottery at Philbrook Art Center."

"Fine exhibit of pottery." *El Palacio* 8:7/8 (July, 1920): 217.

Fine, Robert Ross. "The legacy of Maria Martinez." *Santa Fean* 8:9 (Oct., 1980): 30-34.

Fontana, Bernard L. et al *Papago Indian pottery* Seattle, WA.: Univ. of Washington Press, 1962.

Fox, Nancy. "Pove da, a signature of Maria Martinez." Archaeological Society of New Mexico papers, No. 3 (1976): 259-264.

_____ ."Rose Gonzales" *American Indian Art Magazine.* 2:4 (1977): 52-57.

Frames, Robin. "Pot hunting." *New Mexico Business Journal* (May, 1986): 72-75.

Frank, Larry and Harlow, Francis H. *Historic pottery of the Pueblo Indians, 1600-1880*. Boston, MA.: New York Graphic Society, 1974.

Furst, Peter T. and Jill L. Furst. *North American Indian Art*. New York: Rizzoli, 1982.

G

Germann, F. E. E. "Ceramic pigments of the Indians of the Southwest." *El Palacio* (June 1, 1926): 222-226

Gifford, E. W. *Pottery—making in the Southwest*. Berkeley, CA.: Univ. of California Press, 1928. Publications in American Archaeology and Ethnology Vol. 23 pp. 353-73.

Gill, Spencer. *Pottery treasures, the splendor of Southwest Indian Art*. Portland, OR.: Graphic Arts Center, 1976.

Gladwin, Harold S. *A Method for the designation of Southwestern pottery types*. Globe, AZ.: 1930.

_____.*Some Southwestern pottery types*. Globe, AZ.: 1930-31

Goddard, Pliny Earle. *Pottery of the Southwestern Indians*. New York: American Museum of Natural History, 1931. Guide Leaflet Series No. 73.

Goldsmith, Laura. "Southwest pottery is alive and well." *The Indian Trader* (May, 1981).

A great tradition in pottery." *New Mexico Magazine* 40:4 (April, 1962): 12-13.

Gridley, Marion E. *American Indian Women* New York: Hawthorn, 1974.

_____."Art out of earth; four famous hands that fashion dust into objects of delight." *New Mexico Magazine* 12:11 (Nov, 1934): 7.

Guthe, Carl E. *Pueblo pottery making, a study at the village of San Ildefonso.* New Haven: Yale Univ. Press, 1925. Papers of the Phillips Academy Southwestern Expedition, No. 2.

H

Hale, J. D. "At the Heard: our culture in clay." *Arizona Days & Ways"* (March 14, 1965): 39-43.

Halseth, Odd S. "The revival of pueblo pottery making." *El Palacio* 21:6 (1926): 135-154.

Harlow, Francis H. *Historic Pueblo Indian pottery; painted jars and bowls of the period, 1600-1900.* Santa Fe, NM: Museum of New Mexico Press, 1967.

_____ . _____ . Rev. ed. 1970.

_____ .*Matte-paint pottery of the Tewa, Keres and Zuni Pueblos.* (Santa Fe) Museum of New Mexico Press, 1973.

_____ .*Modern Pueblo pottery: 1880-1960.* Flagstaff, AZ.: Northland Press, 1977.

_____ ."Tewa Indian ceremonial pottery." *El Palacio* 72:4 (1965): 13.

Harlow, Francis H. and Young, John V. *Contemporary Pueblo Indian pottery.* Santa Fe, NM: Museum of New Mexico Press, 1965.

Harlow, Francis H. and Bartlett, Katharine. *Introduction to Hopi pottery.* Flagstaff: Museum Northern Arizona, 1978.

Hartman, Russell P. *Navajo pottery; traditions and innovations.* Flagstaff, AZ.: Northland Press, 1987.

Harvey, B. "Is pottery-making a dying art?" *Masterkey* 38 (Apr.-June, 1964): 55-65.

Hedges, Ken. *Heritage in clay: the 1912 Pueblo pottery collections of Wesley Bradfield and Thomas S. Dozier.* San Diego Musuem papers No. 17, 1984.

Hering, Michael J. "Zia matte-paint pottery: a 300-year history." *American Indian Art.* 12 (4) (1987): 38-45.

Hewett, Edgar L. "Crescencio Martinez - Artist" in *El Palacio* 5:5 (Aug. 3, 1918); 67.

_____.*Native American artists.* Washington, DC: Washington Archaeological Society, 1922.

Hill, W. W. *Navajo pottery manufacture.* Albuquerque: 1937. Univ. of New Mexico Bulletin, Anthropological Series Vol. 2, No. 3.

Hodge, Federick W. "Pottery of Hawikuh" *Indian Notes,* Museum of the American Indian, Heye Foundation. 1:1 (1924): 8-15.

Hodge, Zahrah Preble. "Maria Martinez, Indian Master Potter." *Southern Workman* 62:5 (1933): 213-215.

Holmes, William H. *Pottery.* Washington: Gov. Printing Office, 1912.

_____."Pottery of the Ancient Pueblos." Washington, DC.: Bureau of American Ethnology. Fourth Annual Rept. 1886.

Hoolihan, Patrick. et al *Harmony by hand, art of the Southwest Indians, basketry, weaving, pottery.* San Francisco, CA: Chronicle Books, 1987.

Hough, Walter. *The Hopi Indian Collection in the U.S. National Museum.* Washington, DC: Smithsonian Institution, 1918.

"How Pueblo Indian pottery is fired." *School Arts Magazine* 49:3 (Nov. 1949): 90a

Howard, Richard M. "Contemporary Pueblo Indian Pottery" in *Ray Manley's Southwestern Indian Arts & Crafts*, 1975. 33, 35-52.

Hyde, Hazel. *Maria making pottery*. Santa Fe: Sunstone Press, 1973.

_____ . _____ . Rev. ed. Santa Fe: Sunstone Press, 1983.

I

"Indian pottery from cooking ware to fine art" *The Santa Fean* 2:1 (Dec.-Jan., 1974): 18-19.

J

Jacka, Jerry and Gill, Spencer. *Pottery treasures, the splendor of Southwest Indian art*. Portland, OR: Graphic Arts Center, 1976.

James, Marjorie. "A note on Navajo pottery making." *El Palacio* 43: 13-15 (1937) 85-86.

Jeancon, Jean A. *Santa Clara and San Juan Pottery*. Denver: Denver Art Museum, 1931.
Leaflet 35.

Jeancon, Jean A. and Douglas, Frederic H. *Hopi Indian pottery*. Denver: Denver Art Museum, 1932.
Leaflet 47.

Jeancon, Jean A. and Douglas, Frederic H. *Pueblo Indian pottery making* Denver: Denver Art Musuem, 1935.
Leaflet 6

K

Kabotie, Fred. *Designs from the ancient Mimbrenos with a Hopi interpretation*. Flagstaff, AZ.: Northland Press, 1982.

Kayser, David W. "Take a smooth pebble, add hard work: that's Maricopa pottery." *El Palacio* 77:1: 25-32.

Kidder, Alfred Vincent. *Pottery of Pajarito Plateau and some adjacent regions in New Mexico.* Lancaster, PA: Memoirs of the American Anthropological Association, 1915.

Kidder, Alfred Vincent. *Pottery of the Pecos.* Vol. 1 New Haven: Yale Univ. Press, 1931:
Papers of The Phillips Academy Southwestern Expedition, No. 5.

Kidder, Alfred Vincent and Kidder, M.A. "Notes on the pottery of the Pecos." *American Anthropologist* N.S. 19:3 (1917): 325-360.

Kidder, Alfred Vincent and Shepard, A.O. *The pottery of Pecos.* Vol. 2 New Haven: Yale Univ. Press, 1936.

ACOMA POLYCHROME JAR

Black and red on white; red base. 11-1/4 inches high,
13-1/2 inches diameter. Collections of the Museum of New Mexico.

L

Laboratory of Anthropology, Santa Fe, New Mexico. *I am here.* Santa Fe, NM: Museum of New Mexico Press, 1989.

La Farge, Oliver. *A pictorial history of the American Indian.* New York: Crown, 1956.

Lambert, Marjorie F. *Pueblo Indian pottery: materials, tools, and techniques.* Santa Fe: Museum of New Mexico Press, 1966.
Museum of New Mexico Press Popular Series Pamphlet No. 5.

Le Blanc, Steven A. *The Mimbres people: ancient Pueblo painters of the American Southwest.* London: Thames and Hudson, 1983.

LeFree, Betty. *Santa Clara pottery: the story of an ancient craft:* Albuquerque: Univ. of New Mexico Press, 1974.

_____.*Santa Clara pottery today.* Albuquerque: Univ. of New Mexico Press, 1975.

Lemos, Pedro J. "The household arts of the Indian Pueblos." *El Palacio* 16:8 (April 15, 1924): 127-129.

Link, Martin. "Lucy Martin Lewis: American Indian pottery" *Indian Trader* 15 (11): (Nov. 1984): 4-8.

_____."Potter Mary Small: a hot name in ceramics." *Indian Trader* 16 (8): (Aug. 1985): 3,5.

Lister, Robert H. and Lister, Florence C. *Anasazi pottery.* Albuquerque: Univ. of New Mexico Press, 1978.

Lister, Robert H. and Lister, Florence C. *The Earl H. Morris memorial pottery collection, an example of ten centuries of prehistoric ceramic art in the Four Corners country of the Southwestern U.S.* Boulder, CO.: Univ. of Colorado Press, 1969.
Univ. of Colorado studies in Anthropology, No. 16.

Lyon, Dennis. "Collecting" in *Ray Manley's Southwestern Indian Arts & Crafts*. 1975. p. 34.

_____ ."The polychrome plates of Maria and Popovi." *American Indian Art Magazine* 1:2 (Feb., 1976): 76-79.

Lyon, Luke. "Black or red?" *New Mexico Magazine* 65:8 (August, 1987): 50-55.

M

McCoy, Ronald. "Southwestern pottery: new forms, old legends." *Craft International* Vol. 6, No. 2 (July-August-Sept. 1987): 20-21.

McGreevy, Susan Brown. *Maria: The Legend, the legacy.* Santa Fe, NM: Sunstone Press, 1982.

Mails, Thomas E. *The Pueblo of the earth mother.* Garden City, NY: Doubleday, 1983.

"Maria and Julian Martinez." *School Arts* 49:3 (Nov., 1949): 100.

"Maria, Potter-Teacher." *The Atom* 1:5 (May, 1964): 12-15.

Marriott, Alice. *Maria, the potter of San Ildefonso.* Norman: Univ. of Oklahoma Press, 1948.

_____ ._____. Reprinted 1976, 1987.

Maxwell Museum of Anthropology *Seven Families in Pueblo Pottery.* Albuquerque; Univ. of New Mexico Press 1974, 1980.

Mera, Harry Percival. *The "Rain Bird," a study in Pueblo design.* Santa Fe: Laboratory of Anthropolgy, 1937. (Memoirs of Lab. of Antoropology, Vol. 2)

_____ .*Pueblo designs, 176 illustrations of the "Rain Bird."* New York: Dover, 1970.
". . . an unabridged republication of the work originally published by the Laboratory of Anthropology. Santa Fe, New Mexico, in 1937 . . . with the title The *"Rain Bird"*, a study in Pueblo design.

_____ .*Style trends of Pueblo pottery in the Rio Grande and Little Colorado cultural areas from the sixteenth to the nineteenth century.* Santa Fe: Laboratory of Anthropology, 1939. Memoirs of the Laboratory of Anthropology, V. 13.

Miller, Marjorie. *Indian Arts and Crafts.* Los Angeles: Nash, 1972.

Minor, Marz and Minor, Nono. *The American Indian Craft book.* Lincoln: University of Nebraska Press, 1972.

Monthan, Guy. "Helen Cordero" *American Indian Art Magazine* 2:4 (1977): 72-76.

Morris, Earl H. "The Beginnings of pottery making in the San Juan area: unfired prototypes and the wares of the earliest ceramic period." American Museum of Natural History Anthropological Papers 28 (1927): 125-198.

Moulard, Barbara L. *Within the underworld sky: Mimbres ceramic art in context.* Pasadena, CA: Twelve trees Press, 1984.

Mulberger, Linda and Mulberger, Michael. *Ageless images of Southwestern pre-historic pottery.* Scottsdale: M. Mulberger, 1980.

Museum of Northern Arizona. *An introduction to Hopi pottery* Flagstaff, AZ.: 1978.

Museum of Northern Arizona. *Navajo pottery.* Flagstaff, AZ.: 1987.

Musial, Jan, Editor. *Navajo pottery; traditions and innovations.* Flagstaff, AZ.: Northland Press, 1987.

N

Naylor, Maria *Authentic Indian designs*. New York: Dover, 1975.

Nelson, Mary Carroll. *Maria Martinez* Minneapolis, MN.: Dillon, 1972.

_____ ."Modern guild, ancient arts." *New Mexico Magazine* 56:5 (May, 1978): 26-31.

_____ .*Pablita Velarde* Minneapolis, MN: Dillon, 1971.

New Mexico Association on Indian Affairs. *Indian pottery by the roadsides*. Santa Fe: (193-?). "Published with the approval of the Laboratory of Antropology, Santa Fe, New Mexico." No. 5, Indian Art Series.

New Mexico Magazine *The Indian Arts of New Mexico*. Santa Fe, NM.: 1975.

Reprinted features from New Mexico Magazine.

O

Oleman, Minnie. *"Lucy Lewis: Acoma's versatile potter."* El Palacio. 75:2 (Summer, 1968): 10-12.

Otis, Raymond. *Indian Art of the Southwest*. Santa Fe: Southwest Indian Fair, 1931.

P

Peckham, Stewart. "The beginnings of a tradition — pottery making comes to the Southwest." *El Palacio* V. 93: No. 1 (Summer/Fall, 1987): 20-23.

Peterson, Susan. *The living tradition of Maria Martinez*. Tokyo, New York: Kodansha, 1977.

_____ .*Lucy M. Lewis: American Indian Potter.* New York, NY.: Kodansha, 1984.

_____ .*Maria Martinez, five generations of potters.* Washington, DC: Published for the Renwick Gallery of the National Collection of Fine Arts by the Smithsonian Institution Press, 1978. "Published on the occasion of an exhibition at the Renwick Gallery . . . March 31 - August 6, 1978."

_____ ."Matriarchs of Pueblo pottery." *Portfolio* 2:5 (Nov./Dec., 1980): 50-55.

Philbrook Art Center. *Indian pottery of the Southwest in the Post Spanish period.* Tulsa, OK.: 1960.

Philbrook Art Center. *Native American Art at Philbrook.* Tulsa, OK.: 1960.

"Poh-we-ka (Little Blue Corn Flower)." *El Palacio* 6:7 (March 22, 1919): 98.

The pottery jewels of Joseph Lonewolf. Scottsdale, AZ.: Dandick, 1975.

"Pueblo New Mexico Pottery." *El Palacio* 16:10 (May 15, 1924): 157.

"Pueblo pottery of New Mexico." *El Palacio* 82:3 (Fall, 1976): 2-52.   Note: An errata notice appears in 82:4 (Winter, 1976): 48.

R

Reynolds, Dorothy. "Pottery makers of the pueblos." *School Arts Magazine* 35:3 (Nov., 1935) 205-211.

Rodee, Marian and Ostler, James. Zuni pottery. West Chester, PA.: Schiffer Publications, 1986.

Rogers, Malcolm J. "Yuman pottery making." San Diego Museum Papers No. 2, 1936.

S

Saunders, Charles F. "The Ceramic art of the Pueblo Indians." The International Studio 41:163 (Sept., 1910): 56-70.

Sayles, Gladys and Sayles, Ted. "The Pottery of Ida Redbird." Arizona Highways 24 (1948): 28-31.

Schlager, Ann P. An illustrated guide to Pueblo Indian pottery. 1900-1975. Lawrence, Museum of Anthropology, University of Kansas, 1980.

School Arts. V. 49:3 (Nov., 1949). Entire issue.

Schroeder, Gail P. "San Juan pottery: methods and incentives." El Palacio 71:1 (Spring, 1964): 45-51.

Seton, Julia M. American Indian Arts, a way of life. New York: Ronald Press, 1962.

Sides, Dorothy Smith. Decorative Art of the Southwestern Indians. New York: Dover, 1961.
"An unabridged and corrected republication of the work originally published in portfolio format by the Fine Arts Press, Santa Ana, California, in 1936."

Smith, Mrs. White Mountain. "Lena Blue Corn — potter of Hopiland." The Desert Magazine 2:12 (Oct., 1939): 18-20.

Spinden, Herbert J. "The making of pottery at San Ildefonso." The American Museum Journal. 11:6 (1911).

Spivey, Richard L. Maria. Flagstaff, AZ.: Northland Press, 1979.

Spivey, Richard L. "Signed in clay." El Palacio 86:4 (Winter, 1980-81): 8-9.

Stiles, Helen E. *Pottery of the American Indians.* NY.: Dutton, 1939.

Summer, Polly. "A Margaret Tafoya retrospective." *New Mexico Magazine.* (June, 1983): 21.

Sundt, William M. "*Design analysis of a pure variety of Santa Fe black on white*" Archaeological Society of New Mexico. Papers No. 9, 1984. pp. 13-35.

T

Tanner, Clara Lee. "Crafts of Arizona Indians." *Arizona Highways.* (July, 1960): 8-25.

_____."The Evolution of Southwest Indian Pottery." *Phoenix Magazine.* (May, 1975).

_____."Pottery of the modern Southwestern Indians." *Kiva* (Nov., 1944): 3-12.

_____.*Prehistoric Southwestern craft arts.* Tucson, AZ.: Univ. of Arizona Press, 1976.

_____.*Southwest Indian craft arts.* Tucson: Univ. of Arizona, 1968.

_____."Southwest painted pottery. II, The historic period." *Arizona Quarterly* (Summer, 1947): 138-150.

_____.*et al Ray Manley's Collecting Southwestern Indian Arts & Crafts.* Tucson, AZ.: Ray Manley Photography, Inc. (n.d.)

"Three steps in making Zia pottery." *School Arts Magazine.* 49:3 (Nov., 1949): 90b.

Tierney, G. "Of pots and plants." *El Palacio* (Fall, 1976): 48-52.

Toulouse, Betty. "Maria - the right woman at the right time." *El Palacio* 86:4 (Winter 1980-81): (3)-7.

_____ .*Pueblo pottery of the New Mexico Indians: ever constant, ever changing.* Santa Fe: Museum of New Mexico Press, 1977.

Trimble, Stephen. *Talking with the clay: The art of Pueblo pottery.* Santa Fe, NM.: School of American reserach, 1987.

Trucco, Terry. "Pond Lily has them lining up." *Art News* 80:2 (Feb., 1981): 26.

Tryk, Sheila. "Solving the Pecos pottery mystery." *New Mexico Magazine.* 57:7 (July, 1979): 20-23.

Tschopik, Harry S., Jr. *Navaho pottery making; an inquiry into the affinities of Navaho painted pottery.* Cambridge, MA.: Peabody Museum of American Archaeology and Ethnology, 1941.
Papers of the Museum, Vol. 17, No. 1.

_____ ."Taboo as a possible factor involved in the obsolescence of Navaho pottery and basketry." *American Anthropolgist* 40:2 (1938): 257-62.

U

Underhill, Ruth. *Pueblo crafts.* Phoenix, AZ.: U.S. Indian Service, Education Division, 1944.
Indian Hand Crafts, 7.

V

Vaillant, George C. *Indian Arts of North America* New York: 1939.

Voll, Charles B. *The glaze paint ceramics of Pottery Mound, New Mexico.* Albuquerque: University of New Mexico, 1961.
Thesis — MA.

W

Wade, Edwin L. "The Thomas Keam collection of Hopi pottery: a new typology." *American Indian Art Magazine* 5:3 (1980): 54-61.

Walker, Willard and Wyckoff, Lydia L. *Hopis, Tewas and The American Road* Middletown, CT.: Wesleyan Univ., 1983.

Ward, Bob. "An ancient art is a thriving art in New Mexico."*The Indian Trader* (Spet., 1974).

_____."Pueblo pottery." *New Mexico Magazine.* 52:56 (1974): 23-30.

Warren, A.H. *The pottery of Los Esteros.* 1976.

Watkins, T.H. "Legacy of Hands." *American Heritage* 29:6 (Oct., 1978): 36-37.

Westlake, Inez B. *American Indian designs.* 1st. series. New York: Perleberg, 1925.

_____._____. 2nd. series. Philadelphia: Perleberg, 1930.

Whiteford, Andrew Hunter *North American Indian Arts* New York: Golden Press, 1970.

_____.*North American Indian Arts and Crafts.* New York: Western, 1970.

Whitman, William *The Pueblo Indians of San Ildefonso, a changing culture.* Col. Univ. Pr. 1947. New York: Columbia Univ. Contributions to Anthropology, No. 34.

Wilks, Flo. "Maria revisited." *New Mexico Magazine* 54:5 (May, 1976): 30-32.

Wilson, Eva *North American Indian designs for artists and craftspeople.* New York: Dover, 1987.

Wilson, Olive "The Survival of an American Art." *Art and Archaeology* 9:1 (1920): 24-28.

Winter, Annette "Lucy's legacy." *Modern Maturity* 30:4 (Aug.-Sept., 1987): 42-43.

Wormington, H. M. and Arminta, Neal. *The story of Pueblo pottery*. Denver: Denver Museum of Natural History, 1951. Museum Pictorial No. 2.

Wright, H. Diane. "Navajo pottery: contemporary trends in a traditional craft." *American Indian Art Magazine* 12:2 (Spring, 1987): 26-35.

Z

Zebrowski, Jeanne-Marie. "The Marketplace: what pot? Ancient, old, or new Southwest Indian ware." *American Art & Antiques* 2:5 (Sept.-Oct., 1979): 35, 126, 129-136.

ZUNI POLYCHROME JAR

Black and red on white; black base. Features deer with "heart line". 9-1/2 inches high, 12-1/2 inches diameter. Collections of the Museum of New Mexico.

NOTES

www.ingramcontent.com/pod-product-compliance
Lightning Source LLC
Chambersburg PA
CBHW022343280326
41934CB00006B/763